CPSIA information can be obtained
at www.ICGtesting.com
Printed in the USA
LVHW01s1804130918
590068LV00004B/717/P

D1112005

Psychic Photograph of W. T. Stead given at Crewe, 1915.
See Introduction.

THE BLUE ISLAND

Given by W. T. STEAD through Automatic Writing
to MR. PARDOE WOODMAN in sittings with MISS
ESTELLE STEAD.

Introductory Letter by
SIR ARTHUR CONAN DOYLE

A graphic account of the great sea disaster, the
sinking of the *Titanic*, and its effect on the victims,
with their arrival on the *Blue Island* and the wonderful preparations of the spirit friends for their
reception and entertainment in relieving them from
the shock and sorrow of the tragedy. The wisdom
of the great leader shines thru every page.
—*The Publishers.*

Martino Publishing
Mansfield Centre, CT
2014

Martino Publishing
P.O. Box 373,
Mansfield Centre, CT 06250 USA

ISBN   978-1-61427-566-4

© *2014   Martino Publishing*

Cover design by T. Matarazzo

Printed in the United States of America On 100% Acid-Free Paper

THE BLUE ISLAND

Given by W. T. STEAD through Automatic Writing to MR. PARDOE WOODMAN in sittings with MISS ESTELLE STEAD.

Introductory Letter by
SIR ARTHUR CONAN DOYLE

A graphic account of the great sea disaster, the sinking of the *Titanic,* and its effect on the victims, with their arrival on the *Blue Island* and the wonderful preparations of the spirit friends for their reception and entertainment in relieving them from the shock and sorrow of the tragedy. The wisdom of the great leader shines thru every page.

—The Publishers.

Published and for sale by
THE AUSTIN PUBLISHING CO.
LOS ANGELES   CALIFORNIA

CONTENTS

LETTER FROM SIR ARTHUR CONAN DOYLE

I found the narrative most interesting and helpful. I have no means of judging the exact conditions under which it was produced, or how far subconscious influences may have been at work, but on the face of it, speaking as a literary critic, I should say that the clear expression and the happy knack of similes were very characteristic of your father. We have to face the difficulty that the details of these numerous descriptions of the next spheres differ in various MSS., but on the other hand, no one can deny that the resemblances far exceed the differences. We have to remember that the next world is infinitely complex and subdivided —"My Father's house has many mansions"—and that, even in this small world, the account of two witnesses would never be the same. If a description were given by an Oxford don, and also by an Indian peasent, their respective stories of life in this world would vary much more than any two accounts that I have ever read of the world to come. I have specialized in that direction—the

physical phenomena never interested me much—
and I can hardly think that anyone has read more
accounts, printed, typed and written, than I have
done, many of them from people who had no idea
what the ordinary spiritualist scheme of things
might be. In some cases the mediums were children. Always there emerges the same idea of a
world like ours, a world where all our latent capa-
bilities and all our hidden ambitions have free and
untrammelled opportunities. In all there is the
same talk of solid ground, of familiar flowers and
animals, of comfortable homes, or human pleasures, of congenial occupation—all very different
to the vague and uncomfortable heaven of the
Churches. I confess that I cannot trace in any of
these any allusion to a place exactly correspond-
ing to this Blue Island, though the color blue is,
of course, that of healing, and an island may be
only an isolated sphere—the anti-chamber to others.
I believe that such material details as sleep, nourish-
ment, etc., depend upon the exact position of the
soul in its evolution, the lower the soul the more
material the conditions. It is of enormous importance that the human race should know these things,
for it not only takes away all fear of death, but it
must, as in the case of your father, be of the very
greatest help when one is suddenly called to the
other side, and finds oneself at once in known surroundings, sure of one's future, instead of that
most unpleasant period of readjustment, during
which souls have to unlearn what their teachers

here have taught and adapt themeslves to unfa-
miliar facts.

Good luck to your little book.

Crowboro',
September, 1922.

ARTHUR CONAN DOYLE.

PREFACE

WHEN in April, 1912 the *Titanic* sank in mid-ocean and my father passed on to the next world, I was on tour with my Shakespearean Company. Amongst the members of that Company was a young man named Mr. Pardoe Woodman, who on the very Sunday of the disaster foretold it as he sat talking after tea. He did not name the boat or my father, but he got so much that pointed to disaster at sea and the passing on of an elderly man intimately connected with me, that when the sad news came through we realized he must have been closely in touch with what was about to happen. I mention this incident because it formed the first link between my father and Mr. Woodman, and as it is largely due to Mr. Woodman's psychic powers that my father had been able to get through the messages which are contained in this book, I think, therefore, it will be of interest to readers and should be put on record.

A fortnight after the disaster I saw my father's face, and heard his voice just as distinctly as

I heard it when he bade me good-bye before em-
barking on the *Titanic*. This was at a sitting with
Mrs. Etta Wriedt, the well-known direct voice
medium. At this sitting I talked with my father
for over twenty minuets. This may seem an amazing assertion to many, but it is a fact vouched for
by all those who were present at the sitting. I
put it on record at the time in an article published in *Nash's Magazine,* which included the signed
testimonies of all those present.

From that day to this I have been in constant
touch with my father. I have had many talks with
him and communications from him containing
very definite proofs of his continued presence
among us. I can truly say that the link between
us is even stronger to-day than in 1912, when he
threw off his physical body and passed on to the
spirit world. There has never been a feeling of
parting, although at first the absence of his physical presence was naturally a source of very great
sadness.

In 1917, Mr. Woodman was invalided out of
the army and came to stay with us at our country
cottage at Cobham. Whilst with us, the news came
to him that his great friend had been killed at the
Front, and his interest in the possibility of communication with the next world, which had been
indifferent till then, became intense, and he set
out to find out for himself. It is ever the passing
on of a loved one that gives the necessary stimulus
for eager enquiry.

It was not long before his friend was able to give him definite proof of his continued existence and of his ability to communicate. His first proofs were given through Mr. Vout Peters, and were followed by others through Mrs. Leonard's mediumship and through the mediumship of friends gifted with psychic powers. I was present at that first sitting with Mr. Peters, father was there also, and his friend said it was due to my father's presence and help that he was able to succeed so well in these first attempts at communication.

Shortly after this Mr. Woodman found that he himself had the power of automatic writing and father and others were soon able to write through him. Father always prefers me to be present, and if I am not he seems to have more difficulty, and very rarely will attempt writing. He explains the necessity of my presence in this way: he and I are so much *en rapport*, and so closely in touch with each other that he is able to draw much power from me; I act as the connecting link and form a sort of battery between him and Mr. Woodman. I merely sit passively by whilst Mr. Woodman writes. Generally I see a light around us, and a strong ray of light concentrating on Mr. Woodman's arm. Sometimes I am able to see father himself and always, when he is writing, I feel his presence very distinctly.

We have received many messages in this way. For a while in 1918 we sat regularly every week, and were kept in touch with much that is going on at the Front and of what was about to happen, and were advised of occurrences, often days before the news came through in the ordinary way. In one case father gave us the actual headlines which would (and did) appear in the papers the following week.

It is interesting and also of importance to note that Mr. Woodman and my father met only once before the passing of the latter. I introduced Mr. Woodman to him not long before he left England on the *Titanic*, and they only exchanged two or three words. Therefore Mr. Woodman never knew my father personally nor has he come into touch with his writings or with his work in any way, and yet the wording and the phrasing of the messages are my father's, and even the manner of writing is typical of him.

Mr. Woodman always writes with his eyes closed, and often holds a handkerchief over them. Some of the best messages were given in the twilight when it was impossible for me to follow what was being written, and yet the words were never overwritten. The writing will stop whilst father evidently reads over what has been written, and alterations will be made, "i's" dotted and "t's" crossed correctly. It was a habit of my father's, whilst here, to go back over his copy and cross his "t's" and dot his "i's;" this habit was only known to a few, and was certainly absolutely unknown to Mr. Woodman.

Two of the messages in this way have already been published. They were given by my father

for Armistice Day, 1920, and Armistice Day 1921.
For the first, we had no idea he contemplated
giving a message. A few friends, including Mr.
Woodman, were taking tea with my mother and
myself on the Sunday before the 11th of Novem-
ber. We had been chatting on various subjects,
when I suddenly felt my father come into the room
and could tell by the feeling he gave me that he
wished us to give him an opportunity to write, and
that it was urgent. It was impossible to arrange
for that evening, so we made an appointment for
the evening following. Mr. Woodman came about
nine o'clock. We sat chatting by the fire for a few
minutes; then we felt father come in, and we sat
at once. Father's manner was exactly as it used
to be when here in the body, and he wanted to get
something important done. He must concentrate
on that and on nothing else. Directly we sat, Mr.
Woodman's hand began to move, and father wrote
words to this effect: "I have my message ready,
and if you do not interrupt I hope to succeed in
getting it through." He wrote at tremendous
speed, and in about half an hour had given his
message. Having finished, he gave directions that
it should be read through and punctuated, if necessary. Then left us, not a word about anything
else. It was a strenuous half-hour for us all, but
it was worth it. The message was printed the
next day and many thousands distributed to those
visiting the Cenotaph that year. The 1921 message
was given in the same manner, and thousands of

copies of the two messages, now printed in pamphlet form, were distributed on Armistice Day, 1921.

It was soon after giving this message, that father expressed the wish that we would sit for the messages given in this book. We had felt for some time that he was wanting us to sit for a series of messages, but asked that if this were so he would give us definite instructions to this effect from an outside source. This he did by asking Mrs. Kelway-Bamber, the author of "Claude's Books," at a sitting which she was having with Mrs. Leonard, to tell us that it was quite true he did wish us to sit for a series of messages which, he said, would tell us of his arrival and some of his experiences on the Other Side.

Both Mr. Woodmen and I are busy people, and can only give what spare time we have from our ordinary work to psychic matters, so that it is difficult to fit in times; therefore it was a few months before we had finished taking the messages. These were all given in the manner already described. They were not given consecutively, but definite instructions were given as to how the whole series was to be arranged.

Father's Foreword explains his object in writing this book, so there is no need to dwell on that here. When he started, he had a rather longer book in view, but decided later in favour of a short book as it is more likely to be read, can be published at a reasonable price, and so stand the chance of reaching more people. All who worked

with my father here will know that such reasoning
was characteristic of him.

The photograph given as frontispiece to this
volume was taken by the Crewe Circle at Crew in
the autumn of 1915.   In the spring of that year I
had met Mr. Hope and Mrs. Buxton at the house
of a mutual friend in Glasgow, and they very
kindly invited me to call and see them in Crewe,
if I should ever have an opportunity to do so.   Soon
after my return to London father asked me to arrange to go to Crewe as he said he wanted to try
and give me his picture on the same plate with
mine.   Accordingly I arranged to spend a week-end
with some friends at Crewe and have some sittings
with Mr. Hope and Mrs. Buxton.

I bought a box of plates in London and took
them with me, and I can truthfully say that that
box of plates never left my sight or my possession
all the time I was there.   I even slept with the box
clasped tightly in my hands.   We had our first sitting on Saturday, when I obtained two extras,
neither resembling my father.   One was of interest
because it was the picture of a lady who had appeared on a plate with my father when he was ex-
perimenting with Mr. Boursnell in the nineties.
I took my box containing the rest of the plates
away with me after the sitting; bought another box
of plates in Crewe and took both boxes with me to
the sitting on the Sunday.   We did not use my first
box at all at this sitting, and I kept it all the while
just inside my dress.   We sat around the table,
putting our hands over and under the second box

for a few minutes; I then held the box for a minute
against Mrs. Buxton's forehead. After this I was
instructed by Mr. Hope's guide to take the box myself into the dark room (note, the box had not been
unsealed or the plates exposed to the light). When
in the dark room, I was to unseal the box and take
out the two bottom plates, taking particular care
to note which was the bottom plate, and then to
develop both plates. Mr. Hope was to come in
with me, but not to touch box or plates. I carried
out instructions. I found the bottom plate not even
fogged, and on the other plate two messages, one
from Archdeacon Colley, deploring father's in-
ability to write; one from Mr. Walker, the father
of my host, and in one corner of the plate a faint
outline of my father's face. When I got back to
my friends that evening, we had a sitting at which
father expressed his keen disappointment at his
failure to give his picture. "It is all my fault,"
he said. "I am so excited at the idea of getting
my picture beside yours after I have been so-
called 'dead' for so many years that I break the
conditions; however, many have promised to help
me to-morrow, and if I fail again we have something else prepared to slip on so that you will not
be quite so disappointed." On the following morn-
ing I went for my last sitting. Two of my own
plates were used. On both there are pictures of my
father; one is reproduced in this book, the other
is large face of father which completely covers me.

Now having, I hope, given a little idea as to
how these messages were obtained, and our rea-

sons for feeling that they do indeed come from my
father, I am content to let "The Blue Island" do
the rest. I am sure it will interest many, and if
it awakens some to a truer realization of what is
to come, and makes them seek for further definite
proofs themselves, then the three chiefly concerned
in giving these messages to the public—my father,
Mr. Woodman and myself—will be amply satisfied.

                                    E. W. STEAD.

September, 1922.

FOREWORD BY W. T. STEAD

THERE is great trepidation on the part of all the uninitiated when first coming into contact with occult, psychic or unknown forces. In many of life's mysteries there is much pleasure to be had in probing the secret, and the mystery is in itself an incentive to search and to enquire, to overcome the unknown and to gain knowledge on subjects not previously known or proven. This, however, does not seem to apply when dealing with the mysteries surrounding the after-life. There is always a fear of something. Frequently personal, but sometimes fear of harming the individual known and loved on earth. In itself that is a good sign; it argues unselfishness, and consequently the individual who holds off for that reason deserves enlightenment. If he is sufficiently advanced to seek, he will get enlightenment together with great help. Again, there are those who, imbued with theosophical ideas, fear to come in contact with what is to their minds the shell of a former loved one, and those who fear through ignorance due to an undeveloped and somewhat uneducated mentality. By that

I do not necessarily mean an unschooled mentality.
I speak of "uneducated" in the sense of lacking
understanding and appreciation of the higher
things of life.

To all these people I am, and I always was,
most sympathetic. In earth life I did my best to
help and enlighten, but I was very restricted
owing to material calls upon my time. Since my
arrival in this land I have tried to carry on and
to greatly increase the amount and the sphere of
this same work. I have succeeded up to a point,
though many have not yet reached the half-way
step on that staircase of knowledge leading to
understanding. I was on the point of saying
"leading to happiness," but that would not be
quite correct, for happiness is most amply contained in "understanding," and happiness in the sense
that it is used and understood on earth is *not* the
raison d'etra of life. We were not made only to
be happy. Happiness is part of our reward for
work done, for progress and for help given to
others—which is itself the outcome of understanding.

As I have said, in my work on this side of
the Borderland I have achieved a certain success,
and I am confident that if I can pass on the knowledge I have gained, together with my own personal experiences, to you who are still on earth, I
shall have gone a little larther in the work to
which I have set my hand for the good of human-
ity.

What I have to tell will be of interest to many, and will be useless to many more, but I am going to tell of things which each one of my readers can, up to a point, test for himself. You can each one of you test it by soul knowledge, and by that you will know that I am giving you words of value, words which God in His infinite love has permitted me to be the means of passing to you. It is not *my* idea of the mysteries of life, it is a discourse on those mysteries.

There is the teaching of Christianity running all through, but the application is different to that ordinarily accepted. It is quite erroneous to suppose that because a man was a man on earth, he will become a spirit angel the moment he dies. Death is only the doorway from one room to another, and both rooms are very similarly furnished and arranged. That's what I want you to appreciate thoroughly; it is under the same guiding hand. The same Personality rules in all spheres.

Beginning at the beginning, I have to tell you how a man finds himself here on arrival. As I have said, this whole book will interest many and help a few. It is for that few that all concerned are making the necessary effort to bring it to them. It does not attempt or pretend to be on scientific lines. All through, you can apply sound common-sense, and you cannot break down what is.

I have dealt with the subject very briefly, only for the reason that many will read a short,

concise account who would not study a detailed
one.

I must impress upon you all, the interested
and the disinterested, the believer in this great
subject called "spiritualism" and the sceptic, to
remember you are still on earth and you have still
to perform earth's duties. You have your daily
lives to lead and you must always do well the work
in hand. Never neglect the present because the
future appears more brightly coloured. Carry on
with to-day, but with a corner of your mind on
tomorrow, and remember also that phenomenal
spiritualism is *not* for all. Many minds could not
absorb the greatness of the subject together with
the facts of the phenomena and still continue in
their routine in normal manner—these are the
people for whom phenomenal spiritualism is not.
They will be wise to go no further into the subject than knowledge gained from books and from
the experience of others. In this sense, spiritualism is not for all.

                                          W. T. S.

THE BLUE ISLAND

THE BLUE ISLAND

Experiences of a New Arrival Beyond the Veil

CHAPTER I

THE ARRIVAL

Many years ago I was attracted by an article published on a newly-issued book* on the subject of spirit communication, and after reading the book carefully several times, I was forced to admit its soundness. I was struck by the plain and practical ideas of the writer. That book was the first cause of my becoming actively interested in this big and amazing work. From that time onward I did all in my power to prove and then forward the movement. Many people know this; and those who do not can become acquainted with the details if they wish. Therefore I am going to pass at once from my first earth interest in the occult to my first occult interest in the earth.

---

*Probably "Phantasms of the Living."

Just as I was overcome with astonishment and satisfaction on first reaching conviction on earth, so I was astonished almost equally on my coming to this land and finding that my knowledge of this subject gained on earth was strikingly correct in nearly all the chief points. There was a great satisfaction in proving this. I was at once amazed and delighted to find so much truth in all I had learnt: for although I had believed implicitly, I was not entirely without grave misgivings upon many minor details. Hence my general satisfaction when I recognized things and features which, though I had accepted whilst on earth, I had scarcely anticipated would be as I now found them. This must sound somewhat contradictory, but I want you to understand that my earthly misgivings were based on the fear that perhaps the spirit world had a formula of its own which was quite different to our earth mentality, and that, therefore, the many points were transmitted to us in such a form and in such expression as we on earth would be able to grasp and appreciate, and were not in themselves the precise descriptions, owing to the limitations of earth word-expression.

Of my actual passing from earth to spirit life I do not wish to write more than a few lines. I have already spoken of it several times and in several places. The first part of it was naturally an extremely discordant one, but from the time my physical life was ended there was no longer that sense of struggle with overwhelming odds; but I do not wish to speak of that.

My first surprise came when— I now understand that to your way of thinking I was then dead
—I found I was in a position to help people.
From being in dire straits myself, to being able to
lend a hand to others, was such a sudden transi-
tion that I was frankly and blankly surprised. I
was so taken aback that I did not consider the why
and the wherefore at all. I was suddenly able to
help. I knew not how or why and did not attempt
to enquire. There was no analysis then; that
came a little later.

I was also surprised to find a number of
friends with me, people I knew had passed over
years before. That was the first cause of my
realizing the change had taken place. I knew it
suddenly and was a trifle alarmed. Practically
instantaneously I found myself looking for myself. Just a moment of agitation, momentary only,
and then the full and glorious realization that all
I had learnt was true. Oh, how badly I needed a
telephone at that moment! I felt I could give the
papers some headlines for that evening. That was
my first realization; then came a helplessness—a
reaction—a thought of all my own at home—they
didn't know yet. What would they think of me?
Here was I, with my telephone out of working
order for the present. I was still so near the earth
that I could see everything going on there. Where
I was I could see the wrecked ship, the people,
the whole scene; and that seemed to pull me into
action—I could help! . . . and so in a few seconds
—though I am now taking a long time to tell you,

it was only a few seconds really—I found myself
changed from the helpless state to one of action;
HELPFUL not helpless—I was helpful, too, I think.

I pass a little now. The end came and it was
all finished with. It was like waiting for a liner
to sail; we waited until all were aboard. I mean
we waited until the disaster was complete. The
saved—saved; the dead—alive. Then in one whole
we moved our scene. It was a strange method of
traveling for all of us, and we were a strange
crew, bound for we knew not where. The whole
scene was indescribably pathetic. Many, knowing
what had occurred, were in agony of doubt as to
their people left behind and as to their future
state. What would it hold for them? Would they
be taken to see Him? What would their sentence
be? Others were almost mental wrecks. They
knew nothing, they seemed to be uninterested in
everything, their minds were paralyzed. A
strange crew indeed, of human souls waiting their
ratings in the new land.

A matter of a few minutes in time only, and
here were hundreds of bodies floating in the
water—dead—hundreds of souls carried through
the air, alive; very much alive, some were. Many
realizing their death had come, were enraged at
their own powerlessness to save their valuables.
They fought to save what they had on earth prized
so much.

The scene on the boat at the time of striking
was not pleasant, but it was as nothing to the
scene among the poor souls newly thrust out of

their bodies, all unwillingly. It was both heart-breaking and repellant. And thus we waited—waited until all were collected, until all was ready, and then we moved our scene to a different land.

It was a curious journey that. Far more strange than anything I had anticipated. We seemed to rise vertically into the air at terrific speed. As a whole we moved, as if we were on a very large platform, and this was hurled into the air with gigantic strength and speed, yet there was no feeling of insecurity. . . . We were quite steady. I cannot tell how long our journey lasted, nor how far from the earth we were when we arrived, but it was a gloriously beautiful arrival. It was like walking from your own English winter gloom into the radiance of an Indian sky. There all was brightness and beauty. We saw this land far off when we were approaching, and those of us who could understand realized that we were being taken to the place designed for all those people who pass over suddenly—on account of its general appeal. It helps the nerve-racked new-comer to fall into line and regain mental balance very quickly. We arrived feeling, in a sense, proud of ourselves. It was all lightness, brightness. Everything as physical and quite as material in every way as the world we had just finished with.

Our arrival was greeted by welcomes from many old friends and relatives who had been dear to each one of us in our earth life. And having arrived, we people who had come over from that

ill-fated ship parted company. We were free
agents again, though each one of us was in the
company of some personal friend who had been
over here a long time.

CHAPTER II

THE BLUE ISLAND

I HAVE told you a little about the journey and arrival, and I want now to tell you my first impression and a few experiences. I must begin by saying I do not know how long after the collision these experiences took place. It seemed to be a continuation without any break, but I cannot be certain that this was so.

I found myself in company with two old friends, one of them my father. He came to be with me, to help and generally show me round. It was like nothing else so much as merely arriving in a foreign country and having a chum to go around with. That was the principal sensation. The scene from which we had so lately come was already well relegated to the past. Having accepted the change of death, all the horror of our late experience had gone. It might have been fifty years ago instead of, perhaps, only last night. Consequently our pleasure in the new land was not marred by grief at being parted from earth friends. I will not say that none were unhappy, many were; but that was because they did not understand the nearness of the two worlds; they did not know what was possible, but to those who understood the possibilities, it was in a sense the feeling, "Let us enjoy a little of this new land before mailing our news home;" therefore there was little grief on our arrival.

In writing my first experiences I am going to give a certain amount of detail. My old sense of humour is still with me, I am glad to say, and I know that what I have to say now will cause a certain amount of amusement to those who treat this subject lightly, but that I do not mind. I am glad they will find something to smile at—it will make an impression on them that way, and then when their own time comes for the change they will recognize themselves amongst the conditions of which I am going to write. Therefore to that kind sceptic I just say, "It's all right, friend," and "You give no offence."

My father and I, with my friend also, set out immediately. A curious thing struck me. I was clothed exactly as I had been, and it seemed a little strange to me to think I had brought my clothing with me! There's number one, Mr. Sceptic!

My father was also dressed as I had always known him. Everything and everybody appeared to be quite normal—quite as on earth. We went out together and had refreshment at once, and, naturally, that was followed by much discussion about our mutual friends on both sides. I was able to give them news and they gave me information about our friends and also about the conditions ruling in this new country.

Another thing which struck me was the general colouring of the place; of England it would be difficult to say what the impression of colouring is, but I suppose it would be considered grey-green. Here there is no uncertainty about the impression; it was undoubtedly a blue which predominated. A light shade of a deep blue. I do not mean the people, trees, houses, etc., etc., were all BLUE; but the general impression was that of a blue land.

I commented upon this to my father—who by the way, was considerably more active and younger than he was at the time of death, we looked more like brothers. I spoke of this impression of blue, and he explained that it was so in a sense. There was a great predominance of blue rays in the light and that was why it was so wonderful a place for mental recovery. Now some say, "How completely foolish!" Well, have you not on earth certain places considered especially good for this or that ailment? . . . Then bring common-sense to bear, and realize that the next step after death is only a very little one. You do not go from indifferent manhood to perfect godliness! It is not like that; it is all progress and evolution, and as with people, so with lands. The next world is only a complement of your present one.

We were a quaint population in that country. There were people of all conditions, of all colours, all races and all sizes: all went about freely together, but there was a great sense of caring only for oneself, self-absorption. A bad thing on earth, but a necessary thing here, both for the general and individual good. There would be no progress or recovery in this land without it. As a result of this absorption there was a general peace amongst these many people, and this peace would not have been attained without this self-centerdness. No one took notice of any other. Each stood for himself, and was almost unaware of all the others.

There were not many people that I knew. Most of those who came to meet me had disappeared again, and I saw scarcely any I knew, except my two companions. I was not sorry for this. It gave me more chance of appreciating all this new scene before me. There was the sea where we were, and I and my companions went for a long walk together along the shore. It was not like one of your seaside resorts, with promenade and band; it was a peaceful and lovely spot. There were some very big buildings on our right and on our left was the sea. All was light and bright, and again this blue atmosphere was very marked. I do not know how far we went, but we talked incessantly of our new conditions and of my own folk at home and of the possibility of letting them know how it fared with me, and I think we must have gone a long way. If you can imagine what your world would look like if it were compressed into a place, say, the size of England—with some of all people, all climates, all scenery, all buildings, all animals —then you can, perhaps, form an idea of this place I was in. It must all sound very unreal and dreamlike, but believe me, it was only like being in a foreign country and nothing else, except that is was absorbingly interesting.

I want to give you a picture of this new land without going too deeply into the minute details. We arrived at length at a huge building, circular and with a great dome. Its general appearance was of a dome only—on legs—I mean a great dome supported on vast columns, circular and very big. This again, in the interior, was an amazingly lovely blue. It was not a fantastic structure in any way. It was just a beautiful building, as you have on earth—do not imagine anythink fairylike; it was not. This blue was again very predominant, and it gave me a feeling of energy. I wanted immediately to write. I would like to have been a poet at that moment, but as it was I just wanted to express myself with pen and ink.

We stayed there for some time and had refreshment very similar, it seemed to me, to what I had always known, only there was no flesh food. Everything appeared quite normal there too, and the absence of some things which would on earth have been present was not noticed. The curious thing was that the meal did not seem at all necessary—it was there, and we all partook of it lightly, but it was more from habit than need—I seemed to draw much more strength and energy out of the atmosphere itself. This I attributed to the colour and air. It was while we were in this place that my father explained the reason and work of the different buildings I had noted on our walk together.

CHAPTER III

INTERESTING BUILDINGS

LOOKED upon as a meal—a lunch out—it was the longest one I have ever known and without question the most interesting. I learnt a great deal in those first few hours with my father. It was all conversational, but it was of great use to me and of vast interest. He explained to me that the place we were then in was a temporary rest house, one of many, but the one most used by newly-arrived spirit people. It was nearest to earth conditions and was used because it resembled an earth place in appearance. There were other buildings used for the same purpose as well as for other purposes; by that I mean there is more than *one* of each.

These different houses were not all alike, they varied considerably in outward appearance, but there is no need to describe each. To call it a big building is sufficient, and by that you must understand a place like your museum or your portrait gallery, or your large hotels . . . anything you like, and it is near enough. But it was not fantastic in any way and had no peculiarities, therefore by "building" I mean a building only.

There was a great number of these places in different parts—not grouped together, but variously placed about this land.

It seems that all the senses are provided for here. The chief work on this island is to get rid of unhappiness at parting from earth ties, and therefore, for the time being, the individual is allowed to indulge in most of earth's pleasures. There are attractions of all kinds to stimulate and generally to tone up strength. Whatever the person's particular interest on earth has been, he can follow it up and indulge in it here also for the present. All mental interests and almost all physical interests can be continued here, for that reason of coaxing the newcomer to a level mental outlook.

There are houses given over to book study, music, to athleticism of all kinds. Every kind of physical game can be practiced—you can ride on horseback, you can swim in the sea. You can have all and any kind of sport which does not involve the taking of life. In a minor degree that can be had too, but not in reality; that is only a make-believe.

From this you will understand that particular buildings are given over to their own kind of work. The man who has spent his life in games, heart and soul, would be disconsolate without them here . . . he can have them and enjoy them to the full; but he will find that after a time the desire is not

so keen and he will turn to other interests automatically, though generally, and it may be that he
will never entirely abandon his games, but the
desire will be less absorbing. On the other hand,
the man who used his life for, say, music, for instance, will find his desire, his interest and his
ability increasing by leaps and bounds—because
music belongs to this land. He will find that by
spending much time in one of the music houses, as
he *will* if his life is music, his knowledge and ability are amazingly increased. Then there is the
bookworm. He, too, finds intense satisfaction in
his new-found facilities. Knowledge is unlimited
—works of priceless value, lost upon earth, are in
existence here. He is provided for.

The keen business man on earth whose only
interest is in making his business successful will
also find scope for his ability. He will come in contact with the house of organisation, and he will
find himself linked up with work transcending in
interest anything that he could have imagined for
himself whilst upon earth.

Now all this is done for a reason. Everyone
is provided for. On arriving here there is often
much grief; grief that is sometimes incapacitat-
ing, and no movement forward can be made until
the individual wishes it himself. Progress cannot
be forced upon him. Thus in the scheme of creation the blessed Creator has devised this wonderful
means of appealing to the main interest on earth
of each one. Everyone comes in touch with the
chief longing of earth life, and is given opportun-

ity to indulge in it, and thus progress is assured.

In all things that are purely and solely of the earth, the interest flags after a little time; a reaction, a gradual process—nothing is dramatic here—and the person passes from this to another interest which on earth would be called a mental one. Those whose interests have been in this mind-category will continue and enlarge the scope of their work, and will progress along the same lines —the others change.

Whilst in this Blue Lsland each one is very much in touch with the conditions left behind. At first there is nothing done but what is both helpful and comforting—later there is a refining process to be gone through. At first it is possible to be closely in touch with the home left behind, but after a little time there is a reaction from this desire to be so close to earth, and when that sets in the process of eliminating earth and flesh instincts begins. In each case this takes a different course, a different length of time.

In trying thus to explain the uses of this land and its buildings, I have not numbered them "Building A" for so-and-so, "Building B" for this, that and the other, but, in a conversational way, I hope I have helped you to understand and form a general idea of this country and some of its conditions. I hope I have made it clear how, after a time, the desire for earth things leaves us all. It may be a short or long time, according to the disposition of the person concerned. Take the athlete. He loves his games, his running, his physical strength and his muscular exercise. Well, he will love it here as much. He will love it here more, because he will find an added pleasure in feeling no fatigue, a sharpened enjoyment altogether, but after a time his appreciation of all this will change. He will not dislike this hitherto loved sport, but he will pass to a different form of it. A form which is full of movement and satisfaction but not a physical affair at all; his mind will become more awake, and he will get enormous mental satisfaction from the studies which will come before him concerning the ways and means of travel here. Locomotion of all kinds here is very different to that which obtains in earth conditions, and this former athlete of earth will drop into line in his new surroundings and will presently realize that life here is a different thing for him, for, though on the same lines, it holds an increased mental interest. Is that clear. . . . Well apply it in the same fashion to every other type of individual.

CHAPTER IV

LIFE ON THE ISLAND

HAVING given you a little idea of this land and its appearance, I want to tell you about the life of the people here, so that you can form a mental picture in completeness. It is only natural that many should say, "What are they all doing?" Now, this is a very broad question to answer, and to help you to see how big a thing I am dealing with in thus attempting to give my story of the next life, I must put a simple question to you.

I want you to try and imagine you have not been living on earth and that, knowing nothing of earth life, you have suddenly been landed by an airship in the busiest part of the city of London— with all its traffic and its people. You have arrived from some other world and have not seen this sight before. You will exclaim, "How strange! What are they all doing?" Well, could you answer that question easily? It would not mean much to you to be told they are going about their own individual business—one man bakes

bread, another sweeps the streets, another drives a
cart, and another sits in an office and runs a business—all that would leave you none the wiser.
These are facts, and yet you would not understand
them. You could not comprehend them. That is
my difficulty in trying to make you understand in
a satisfactory way the life of this Blue Isle. I have
to consider how to explain it. It is no use my telling you that one person sits by the sea all the
time, weeping because of her parting from her
lover, and another is in a mental stupor from drink,
and another still thinks he is still ringing the bells
of his local chapel on Sunday, etc., etc.—that is
not the life, those are only bits of it. Atoms of the
whole. I do not want to particularise, I want to
generalise, with one detail. Therefore I must say
that if you were to pay this land a visit in your
earth bodies, as you are at present, you would be
struck by the lack of excitement. You would
think it all so like earth. That is what you would
say to people on your return. "Oh, it's so much
like our life here, only there are such a lot of different races of mankind there."

Everyday life for the individual is strikingly
like the everyday life he's always been used to.
At first he takes a great deal of rest, having the
earth habit of sleep—and it is a necessity—he
needs sleep here too, for the present. We have no
night as you have, but he sleeps and rests just the
same. He has his interests in visiting different
parts, in exploring the land and its buildings and
in studying its animal and vegetable life. He has

friends to seek out and to see. He has his pastimes to indulge. He has his new-found desire for knowledge to feed.

The routine of a day here is similar to the routine of a day on earth; the difference being that earth's routine is often made by force of circumstance, whereas here it is made according to the desire for knowledge on this or that subject.

In closing, we are all practically as on earth and as there are so many races here you can well understand the general appearance of this land is most unusual, and in an odd way particularly interesting and amusing, also instructive. I think I have said that in general appearance we all are as we all were. We are only a very little way from earth, and consequently up to this time we have not thrown off earth ideas. We have gained some new ones, but have as yet discarded few or none.

The process of discarding is a gradual one. As we live here we gain knowledge of many kinds, and come to find so many things, hitherto thought essential, not only of no importance but something of a bore, a nuisance, and that is how we grow to a state of dropping all earth habits. We get to the state of not desiring a smoke, not because we can't have it, or think it not right, but because the desire for it is not there. As with a smoke, so with food, so with many a dozen things; we are just as satisfied without them. We do not miss them; if we did we should have them, and we *do* have them until the desire is no longer there.

At first there is practical freedom of thought and action, and there are only certain limitations imposed—not by rule but by conditions. Beyond these limitations there is absolute freedom. After a time, when the spirit has advanced to the point of desiring knowledge and enlightenment, he will be drawn like a piece of steel to a magnet, into contact with this or that house of organisation dealing with the subject on which he desires knowledge. From the time of coming into touch with this house the spirit will be, as it were, "at school." He will perforce have to attend this house for instruction. He will spend a good deal of his time there learning, and, when finished with one house, will pass to another, but it is not compulsory information, it is craved-for information, and nothing is given until asked for. You are not forced to aquire *anything*. You are more than ever free agents. That is why on earth it is so essential to control your bodies by your minds, and not the reverse. When you come here your mind is all-powerful, and everything depends, for your own degree of happiness here, upon the kind of mind you bring with you.

The presence or absence of contentment is entirely due to the earth life you have led, the character formed, opportunities taken and lost, the motive of and for your actions, the help given, the manner of use of help received, your mental outlook and your use and abuse of flesh power. To sum these all up, it is the quality of mind control over body *versus* body over mind. Mind matters and body matters—on earth. Here only the mind matters, it is in your keeping entirely, and is in whatever state you have made it by your life. On your arrival here the degree of your happiness will be determined automatically by the demands of your mind.

When you are inclined to ask, "What are they all doing there?" turn your mind to some dear one on earth who has taken up an out-of-the-way kind of life somewhere abroad, where you are not in constant and intimate touch, and say to him, "I wonder what he's doing now?" . . . Then answer it yourself by saying, "I suppose he's carrying on." So are we, we people in the Blue Island.

CHAPTER V

INTIMATE LIFE

THERE is a good deal of reasoning and argument as to why in earth life we should do or not do this or that. Why we should refrain from many of the delights of everyday life and why we should "go straight."

People say it is handicapping in their business or their profession to have to observe these "nice points." They may not confess this thought openly, but to themselves they do—they do not see why such and such should not be done. True, they think it may injure so-and-so's business a little, but that is his affair.

All in ignorance.

There is a reason, and that reason can be very easily found by the rule of common-sense. I almost might call this a discourse upon cause and effect.

Earth life has deteriorated. The whole scheme of creation is planned with great precision, with the object of allowing free individual development and progress. Its rules are laid down clearly.

Every man knows by instinct when he is obeying
and when disobeying these rules. It needs no po-
lice officer to tell him. He may deceive himself
that such an act is all that it should be, but at the
same time he knows in his own consciousness that
that act or thought is not only *not* all that it should
be but that it is all that it ought *not* to be. I say
that all mankind knows—but most of mankind
prefer to think it does not know.

Not one person on earth can stand up and say
I am not speaking a profound truth here!

Mostly these things are not considered from
the point of right and wrong, but from the view of,
"shall I benefit from this?"—but I say that *all*
people on earth *can* discriminate, I do not say that
they do, between good and not good motive in their
lives. Instinct does this for them. They cannot
help themselves. They are bound to know. The
trouble is that the vast majority by force of habit,
the desire for business gain, or social gain, or any
kind of gain, but always a gain for itself, has
ceased to consider the quality of its actions and
thinks only of the first result. It is a pity. It is
more than that. Looked upon from the next stage
in evolution it is PITIFUL. Poor undeveloped egos,
preparing their own discomfort and suffering—not
a hell fire but a mental torture.

The self or spirit of a man is encased in his
mind, and, examined in a purely physical way, the
brain is the most baffling organ of the body scientific man ever had to deal with. Much can be understood; all never will be. Judged as being the

casing instrument of the soul it becomes an event
even more delicate and intricate and baffling piece
of work. You all know that mind is the generating
house for all your acts and deeds, but you do not
fully appreciate the fact that every act and every
thought is"booked"—is recorded.

You do not see the elaborate scheme of work
which goes on in any of your large business
houses, when you buy something and do not pay
at once. It is booked and passes through many
hands before the bill is sent to you a little later,
and having paid the bill you forget it all, but the
record of that business house has it still. So with
the brain; an act or a thought, no matter what the
quality, is recorded for all time. Settling will come
after life, and when paid the "book" is finished
with and troubles no more, though the record is
still there. Now follow me. Mind and its work—
thought— is the force that drives and creates everything on earth. It has all to be mental before physical or material. That you all know. Every building was conceived mentally before being built.

Thought is divided in itself into different types.
There is the thought of your next meal, which is
of no particular interest, and there are the thoughts
constructive and destructive. These are important.
There are the purely personal thoughts. Sometimes
advantageous and sometimes the reverse. Now the
all-important forms of thought are the constructive
and destructive. The others referring to your
meals, your clothes, your appearance your anything
you like, these are not of importance until they are

allowed to hinder the flow of constructive thought; when they do this the character of these same thoughts changes and becomes *destructive*.

It is the material embodiment of destructive thought which causes most of the distress and misery in the world. The sum total goes on increasing, and will continue to increase, until mankind as a whole, and individually, will listen and try to understand a little more about himself beyond what it is necessary for him to know for the selling of his goods, and thus give him fuller play to the beneficent action of constructive thought which alone can redeem and save the world.

CHAPTER VI

INTIMATE LIFE *(continued)*

To a great extent the individual hardships of earth life are directly due to wrong thinking. I am fully aware that people are placed in many different positions right from birth. Some inherit unhappiness and difficulty from their parents, and their lot in life is harder and their pleasures are less than in the lives of those who are born in better conditions.

Accepting these differences of position and condition—one man a life of much hard work, another a comfortable and perhaps rather idle life —the same rule of thought applies. The man who has given up under hard conditions is by circumstances forced into a groove of thought—a regular rut. He cannot help himself because there are no real attempts made by any to change his outlook; he may meet with material help from time to time, but he meets with little *practical* mental assistance. He is under the disadvantage of his lifelong earth conditions, and is in ignorance because he does not understand and has little opportunity for learning about these things; by his thought he adds to his difficulties instead of easing and finally removing many of them. The other man, who is comfortably settled and has no particular worries, does precisely the same thing. He trudges along in the same mental rut—stagnation, MENTAL STAGNATION, and the same results will fall to them both hereafter. They are both building up their future states.

Then there are people of keen intelligence clever people, who use their brains to achieve material gain no matter the cost to others. These people are indulging in the most positive form of destructive thought. They are not like the other two, negative. They are very alive, alert and positive. They are at once using destructive and constructive thought. The latter is entirely misapplied, and when they come here the account against them will be much heavier, because they will have built up a wall of greedy thought which they must settle in this next condition.

A thought—no matter the heading it comes under—that has come into your mind and which you have sent out, is an accomplished thing so far as your *mind* goes. Your physical act may or may not keep swift accompaniment with the thought; that does not matter from the point of view of what you are building up for yourself *here*. Once having had this thought it is *done,* so far as your mind is concerned, and, whether you follow it up actively or not, you have to make repayment for

it when you come here. I am not speaking about
the thousand trivial thoughts of every hour, but
about those which I might describe as having personality.

You will say it is impossible to control every
thought of the day, and I agree that it is, but if
once you accepted for fact what I have said, you
would keep a sharp eye on your mental actions.
They matter. You will find this very difficult to
accept because it is indeed an intimate thing for
each one; you do not know each other's thoughts
whilst upon earth, therefore I have headed this
chapter, "Intimate Life."

Each of you will live to thank the person who
is responsible for giving you this information if
you act upon it, and those of you who hear and
know but do not act upon the knowledge, will have
one day to cast reproaches upon yourselves for this
failure.

To realize oneself that one has failed is far
more bitter than the consciousness that others
know it.

Think upon this and reason a little with your
own inner self.

CHAPTER VII

FIRST ATTEMPTS

LEAVING the question of time out of it entirely, as I must, I want to write of my first attempt to communicate with the earth world. I know there is much dissatisfaction with the spirit world on account of the practical impossibility to give correct ideas of time spacing. I should like to say a little about that before going into the main interest of to-day's writing. You must not be over hasty in condemning us for this failure. On earth you all space your time by days and hours, etc., but those spacings are also based, or perhaps more definitely marked in your mental reckoning, by the habits of the day. You have a light sky and a dark sky; without a watch you know fairly accurately the time of day by your inclinations—fatigue or freshness, the need for food or rest, etc., etc.

Now on this side of the grave we have no real necessity for rest or for food. We have no dark sky—only a light one, and we have, for the sake of the present illustration, an unlimited supply of energy. Consequently we are not able to break up the time into spaces which correspond with earth spacings. We do break up our time, but it is not *your* breaking, therefore we can seldom be accurate in telling when a thing did, or when a thing will happen. For that reason I am not able to tell how long I had been in this country before I made my first attempt to link up with earth again. To me I seem to have lived in this land always. It appeared to me that it could be only a few days since I arrived. I had not forgotten by family or my friends, but I felt peculiarly happy about them. I cannot think why, except that finding my earth knowledge so very correct I gathered strength in feeling that they too would understand everything was quite well with me, and that this little delay in writing was natural considering the new country I had come to.

The house which is given over to this work in the Blue Island had been a regular haunting-place of mine ever since my father had told me of it, together with the works of the other buildings. I went to this house a great deal, and received much help from the various people in charge. They were all kind and very sympathetic, but entirely businesslike. It was not merely a house of tears and sympathy, it was an amazingly well organized and businesslike place. There were many hundreds of people there. Those who had on earth believed and those who had not, came to try and wire a message home.

The heart call was the one which received the most serious attention. Many were there only as lookers-on, incredulous and facetious. They got nothing more than the satisfaction of their own amazement.

After a little time my turn came.

For a building given over to this kind of work it appeared to be inadequately equipped. I had rather expected to see many implements and instruments, many wires and machines and the presence of electric forces, but there was nothing of that kind at all and only the human element.

I had a long conversation with a man there —a man obviously of some importance, though I cannot say he looked like an angel, he appeared quite as mundane as myself. I had a long talk with him, and from him heard how a great deal of this work was carried on. He told me they had a system of travellers, whose work was very close to physical earth. They had the power of sensing people who could and would be used for this work at the other end. These men could locate and then tabulate the earth people, marking each individual ability, and when the newly-arrived spirit came in search of help, these sensitives on earth were used as each could be used. This is a sketchy outline of the work done in that building.

. . . There I came frequently and tried to get my messages through to home by more than one means; I succeeded in some ways, I failed in others. The spirit has much to do with himself with the success or failure attained; a great deal depends

upon him.   Every time I succeeded I helped another.   Every time I failed I went myself for help,
and got it.   Having given much time and study to
the subject on earth, I was given unlimited assistance at this end of the line now that I needed it.

I want to explain how I got some of my first
mesages through and how I knew I had succeeded.   We had been taught by this time how to come
in close contact with the earth, although it was not
possible for me to do this alone.   I had a helper
with me.   I must call him an official.   He came
with me to my first trial.

We came into a room which seemed to have
walls made of muslin.   Something and yet nothing.   I knew it was a house, and was conscious of
the walls of the room, and yet they seemed such
poor things because we could see through them
and move through them.   I could not have done
this by myself at that time, but with my official we
did.

Then came the attempt.   There were two or
three people in this room and they were all talking
together about the horror of this great disaster
and about the probability of people coming back.
They were holding a séance and my official show-
ed me how to make my presence known.   The con-
trolling force, he told me, was thought.   I had to
visualize myself among these people in the flesh.
Imagine I was standing there in the flesh, in the
center of them, and then imagine myself still there
with a strong light thrown upon me. . . . Create
the picture.   Hold the visualisation very deliberate-

ly and in detail, and keep it fixed upon my mind, that at that moment I *was* there and that they were conscious of it. I failed, of course, at first, but I know that after a few attempts I succeeded and those people did actually see me. My face only, but that was because in my picture I had seen myself only as a face. I imagined the part they would recognize me by. I was also able to get a message in the same way. Precisely the same way. I stood by the most sensitive present, and spoke and concentrated my mind on a short sentence, and repeated it with much emphasis and deliberation until I could hear part of it spoken by this person. I knew that at last I had succeeded, and I succeeded reasonably easily because I knew so intimately what the conditions of those people and that earth room were. Many who had not my earth knowledge made little impression at all.

There were none of my own family present that time. Had there been it would have made it impossible for me, as I was then feeling their sorrow acutely, and I would not have been able to give my mind so full a power as I did—I became almost impersonal. It was a good thing that my first attempt was purely a test one— to see if I could break through to home.

CHAPTER VIII

THE REALITY OF THOUGHT COMMUNICATION

IN trying to establish a definite form of communication between the earth sphere and the Blue Island, people are always looking for the return of the physical part of the individual. They find it exceedingly difficult to accept even the most pressing mental tests as being a proof of communication; and in giving so much attention to this physical form, they nearly all overlook the form of thought communication, which is much more personal and very much less tainted by outside influences, such as the medium's mind or other sitters . . . antagonism, or bias either way. This thought communication is a much more real form than is accepted by the majority of believers in the possibility of it.

In concentrating the mind on any one spirit person, you are sending out real, live, active forces. These forces pass through the air in precisely the same way as electric waves do, and they never miss their mark. You concentrate on Mr. A. in the spirit world, and immediately Mr. A. is conscious of a force coming to him. In this land we are much more sensitive than whilst on earth, and when thoughts are directed to us by people on your side, we have a direct call from these currents of thought thus generated, and we are practically always able to come in close contact with the person who is thinking of us; when near and acclimatised to his conditions we can impress thoughts and ideas upon his mind. He will seldom accept them for what they are, but will think they are his own normal thoughts or something of an hallucination. Nevertheless, if frequent opportunity is given he will be startled at the amount of information he can record. This applies to everyone, not merely to the believer in these subjects. Anyone who sits for a moment and allows his mind to dwell on some dear one who has "died" will actually draw the spirit of that person to himself. He may be conscious or unconscious of the presence, but the presence is there.

If people on earth realized the result of their thoughts upon those to whom they refer, they would be very much more careful in giving their mind free play. There are so many thoughts possible, and all of them are registered here; many of them affect the people they concern, but all of them affect the people from whom they emanate.

Perhaps in telling you all thoughts are recorded I am making it more difficult for you to accept and understand. It will be better therefore,

to explain that by "all thoughts," I refer only to
"direct" thoughts. In reality every thought is
registered; the personal ones are, as I have previously said, of no importance so long as they are
not allowed to grow into destructive thoughts.

In speaking of direct thought I mean you to
understand *positive* thoughts, about other people,
pleasant or unpleasant, and not the thoughts of
everyday trivialities.

Many people find it impossible to believe that
every direct thought they have is registered, or
that it can in any way influence or affect the person concerned, or return to influence themselves,
but this *is* so.

You are fully aware of the influence given
out by any one person who is deeply depressed or
more than usually excited or happy. Each of you
has felt this influence. This is, of course, caused
by the lowered or raised mental vibrations, giving
out particularly strong currents of either depres-
sion or happiness.

They are equally strong currents in themselves although they act differently upon the people
with whom they come into contact. It is in this
way that all direct thoughts act. Frequently the
subject is not conscious of these thoughts upon
himself, but the influence is there in a subtle and
greater or lesser degree of strength, and all these
thoughts are very definitely registered in the mind
of the thinker, long after the incident has passed.

When coming to this land, that whole record
has to be dealt with. Not by a judge in wig and

gown, but by our own spirit selves. In spirit life we have a full and clear remembrance of all of these things and, according to the quality of these individual thoughts, so we are brought into a state of regret, happiness or unhappiness, despair or satisfaction. It is here that we meet with the desire to make return, to put right all the discomfort and distress, minor or major, as it may be, caused by thoughtless mind action whilst on earth,

This is why I say that whilst o n earth it is not only advisable, but essential, to keep your minds under control and in order. It is only wisdom so to do. The difficulty is that people will not realize this whilst upon earth, alhough they know from their own inner consciousness that I am stating a truth.

I want you all to try and realize the results you are making, the uphappiness you are causing others, and the regret and sorrow you are laying up for yourselves in the next world when you have to face the conditions you have made. Remember that your minds are the generating houses. You are building up whatever is to be your next condition, precisely and exactly by the lives you are leading on earth, by your thoughts and by the degree to which your body controls your mind instead of your mind ruling supreme. So long as you are upon earth you are a Body (Physical) and Soul (Mind) and Spirit (Self). When you come here you are Mind (Soul) and Self (Spirit) only. There fore for your own future happiness it is essential that your Mind should rule during earth life. It is for you to say whether it shall do so. If you are willing to pay your bill when you come over, carry on as you are, but there is no further credit given, you *have* to settle it here. If you are a quarter as practical as you each and all think you are, you will see to it that the mind leads. It can lead very delightfully, although you may think it leads only to religious restriction—it does not only lead there; it leads to all earth's pleasures, all earth's enjoyments, but it always holds the ruling hand, and can stop at the right time, whereas the body cannot, and so it runs up debts which have to be paid, and paid sometimes very dearly and bitterly.

Earth was made beautiful for Man to enjoy—not merely to tantalize him—lead him on and then say "No!" That is not the way of our blessed Creator. He has given beauty and the faculty of enjoying beauty to all mankind, and so long as the mind rules it will continue to be beauty, but only when the body rules, influencing and degrading the mind as it will, then trouble lies ahead. Much trouble and much acute regret.

When we are here our minds work in the same manner, they obey the same rules, and the presence or absence of body does not hinder our thinking powers, and consequently there is no difficulty in coming into touch with some of our people left behind and being in close touch with them, influencing them greatly; although many of them are unconscious of it. I want you to think of this and to realize that your own people can come to you, that thought is all-powerful, and that you can build up or destroy, help or hinder, draw near you, or drive away from you the people incarnate and discarnate, who were and who are so dear to each of you by this power of thought.

Thought communication is the closest link between the two worlds, but it must be well ordered and well trained brain action. You must not imagine that every idea which enters your mind is put there by a spirit person; it is not so at all, but at the same time, if you train your mind in the way an athlete trains his body, you can then ask for and receive great knowledge and much help, both spiritual and material.

CHAPTER IX

POINTS

A SUBJECT of this importance and interest is full of queries. Each one has his own questions to put, and each brings what he considers a hitherto unnoticed point. I want, if possible, to answer a few of these constantly recurring queries now. I had many put to me during my investigations whilst on earth, and some of them I can answer at last. I want you first to realize that by the change of death you *do not* become part of the Godhead *immediately...* The mysteries of life are not revealed to you as a kind of welcoming gift on your arrival here. You must not think that I, or any, have *full* knowledge on all subjects, profound and trivial, the moment we come to spirit life . . . I cannot tell you when your grandson will next require new shoes . . . nor can I tell you the settlement of the Irish question. I can only see a little farther than you, and I do not by any means possess the key to the door of All Knowledge and

All Truth. That, we have each to work for . . . and as we pass through one door we find another in front of us to be unlocked . . . and another, and another.

But, on the other hand, remember that I do know considerably more than you do, because I am in more intimate touch with the Main Source of knowledge and I have passed through an experience which is still ahead of you all.

I should like first to speak about the word "conditions" and its true meaning. It is a word which is grossly misapplied in all forms of psychic work. It is given as a reason for this or that failure—for a success—for any peculiarity in result, and it is looked upon as necessary in any apartment in which a meeting is to be held. Rightly and wrongly—usually wrongly. The main factor or essential in obtaining good results lies in the condition of the sitter's mind more than in the room he is in. The mental attitude and the *physical* state of the sitter is of very much more importance than the presence of draped windows, thick carpets, exotic perfumes, etc., etc., it is the method of mental approach which matters chiefly. That is a feature often overlooked by even the first grade sensitives. . . . Certain "extras" if rightly used and properly directed round the apartment, such as a cheerful face, pleasant flowers, laughter and brightness, these are all quite useful assets, but they are not the essentials.

Some people always try to reduce to ridicule communication with the next world, one of the greatest of God's blessings to mankind, and complain of what they consider to be the senseless conditions ruling at a séance.   Many of these conditions,as I have said, are meaningless and sometimes a hindrance, but at the same time others are necesssary according to the kind of communication sought after.

To make my point, I must recall to you how conditions govern everything, and so much does everything depend upon given suitable conditions, that people do not even notice that this is so.   The simplest and perhaps the most useful example of this, is in making a pot of tea.   You must have the tea in a certain condition—if you do not, you get poor results.   Your flowers—you have your seeds in a certain condition of dryness and you put them to earth when the climate is in a certain condition, according to time of year, and, once planted, you tend your plants, flowers, trees, everything according to the conditions they *demand.*

We demand conditions.   Why should you think that this great scientific work can be governed, mastered by inexperienced hands at any take-it-or-leave-it moment?   You cannot reasonably expect it, and if you do you won't get it!   Conditions govern earth and all forms of life on it, from an earlier state than that when consciousness begins —but I tell you many of the conditions demanded by intelligent workers in this subject are futile, and worse—harmful.   You cannot achieve success in anything, or along any line, by directing your force in opposition to your intelligence.   A vast number do, in this subject, and *that* is why there is so much failure. You may as well try to take a photograph without putting any film into the camera and because you get no result, say the whole thing is impossible and fraudulent. You must have conditions in order to secure success in any and everything. It is due to lack of these necessary conditions that we fail sometimes to influence a person to do or not to do a certain act. A father, in spirit life, may be fully conscious of his son contemplating a certain deed, say, suicide or murder, or anything of that kind. Such knowledge will cause great sorrow to the father, and he will work his utmost to influence the son, to direct his thoughts, and destroy the idea of whatever is contemplated; but at such time the son is in an abnormal state of excitement, which nearly always prevents our influence from getting to him and working upon him. It is not at all a state of happiness for the father, because he is fully aware of his son's acts, and he is powerless to prevent him.

In action we are free. Absolutely free. We have graduated in the Blue School. We are free to go amongst the other spheres. The land where many or several—or none—of our own people are. We can go to them, and we can take help from those more developed, and give help to those less fortunate. Help by advice, help by demonstration, and help by association. We are still living on the Blue Island; not yet do we pass to the next sphere for domicile.

As we are able to travel among these other lands, so we are able to be in constant touch with earth. Thoughts of us sent out by people on earth reach us, and we can sense from whom they come, and can follow up the person, if so desired. We would not get every thought from anyone who happened to see our names and make a casual remark, but from anyone with whom we were intimate whilst on earth a thought of us will come straight, as along a telephone wire from one house to another, and if we wish we can come. In this way we are able to help people left behind. We can follow their actions and their minds, and influence them one way or the other, according to our idea of what is for their good; but we cannot do impossible things even for those dearest to us.

Whilst on earth one can give advice, but one cannot force it into practice—so here we can influence but not create. Having attained this state there is no parting, there is no sting in death, we can be with our own beyond us, with us, below us, and with those still on earth. Separation and parting are not known except by the law of attraction and affection. We leave people behind on earth who dutifully mourn for us, who are genuinely upset at *their* loss—but after a while, short or long—their remembrance of us grows thin. They cease to think of us, to recall us, and to remember our companionship. Those are the only partings. In some cases even those people come back to our lives when they themselves come to this land. Gradually, as they throw off the influence which dimmed their remembrance of us, they find the foundation of the old affection. Sometimes it is untouched; sometimes spoiled; but these are the only partings.

A spirit who comes here, and is anxious to get in touch with earth ties, may be made more unhappy by being with the earth people, for if they do not understand that he is still alive, they are all sadness, and they think of him as dead—as something finished. Although the spirit will go to them a great deal at first, the earth people will not know he is there, and seeing them but being unable to make his presence known causes him much disappointment and sorrow, and gradually he will go to them less and less. Realizing that they are ignorant of his presence and think only of him as dead, he will finally stay away altogether, content to wait until they join him.

This accounts for many people who are not apparently making any attempt to communicate, and for earth people to say that this cannot be true because their dearest so-and-so never made any sign to them.

When you are over in this life you will not be continually associated with people who are not of interest to you. On earth you eliminate, as far as practical, the people who tire and try you—but here that can be done effectively because those feelings and instincts are entirely mutual. The governing force is love. Affections bind people together, and if the love between any two, or any group, is a strong and real thing, then those peo-

ple are in close unison and happiness together.
But wherever the love is not on both or all sides,
there is automatically a falling away of the affect-
ed party. Nothing uneven or unequal holds. When
you come, through death, you are attracted by the
ties of love into the set of people who vibrate the
same affection, and if you have had an affection
for another which is not equally shared, although
you will at first be together, you will gradually and
yet quietly cease to attract each other, and cease
to be in each other's company.

CHAPTER X

THE STATE OF FREEDOM

EVERYTHING is ordered. I have touched lightly
upon my first arrival and my impression of the new
surroundings, and of my first return to earth and
the manner of it. Without giving technical and
scientific formulæ at all, I think I have given you
a fair picture and a rough idea of the next step
after earth life. What I have said applies to all
the human race. Whites, blacks and yellows—
there is no differentiation; one rule holds for all
races of mankind.

I shall pass for the present to a further stage.

I may return to say more about the Blue
Island, but now I will leave all life there to continue on its way, and will deal with a further point
of development—the state of being rid of most of
earth instincts. Once rid of these we are able to
pass with comparative ease, and almost at will,
from one sphere to another and from this or another sphere back to earth; keeping thereby in
close association with our own people—or those of

them who desire it. We help by influencing them
in their daily lives and actions, and we do this
without in any way retarding our own work, de-
velopment and construction of character. Character is the main thing to be studied.

Whilst on the Blue Island I studied, as all do,
the secrets of self and of life, and I came to realize the vastness of Creation. It is not life on
earth and then life on this island only. As progress
is made and earth's inclinations and habits are put
aside, so other interests take their place and then
comes the desire for true knowledge. As others
do and will do, so did I. I fell into line also, and
as I learned so I progressed. Capacity for wisdom
grew with the wisdom acquired

I had learnt of the existence of other lands
besides this island, and at one time it seemed as
incredible as the possible existence of *this* land
does to many now on earth; but eventually the
time came when I was taken to these other spheres.
I cannot tell where they are, but it was like trav-
elling among the stars. It seems as if we left our
world and travelled through space until we reached another star, another land.

There are several of these other lands, and
they are inhabited by former earth people who have
progressed sufficiently to qualify for entry into
this or that land. These other lands are nearly
all inhabited by a higher form of life, a happier
form and, individually, a more powerful form, but
there are one or two other lands of not so high an
order, where happiness is less or not at all, ac-

cording to whether life on earth was a well, or
lightly-ordered thing. In these lands the people
who are there fail and fail again to find the spirit
in themselves to desire to rise, to improve and control themselves, although the necessary strength
is offered and offered and even thrust at them.

All races have the gift of free-will. All are
free agents in determining their own destinies.
At all times, not only after the body's death. Just
as a father and a mother of a family order the
day's routine for their children, and allow the children then to amuse themselves in their own way,
so the races of mankind are free to develop their
lives upon their own individual pattern—being
given certain rules to conform to. All life is
originally free but whilst on earth, through poor
comprehension and mismanagement, the individual often thinks he is not a free personage with free
will—but he *is*. As the same father and mother
will influence and guide their children, the cause
being love, so when we are here and find ourselves
able, we do our utmost to help and influence those
we love who are still on earth. Always it is the
driving force of love which causes us to do our
work.

We can be in close touch with our people on
earth, and by suggestion and by close association
we can influence them. Through our influences often
much material good will come to them. We spirit
people cannot give material riches to *any* on earth,
but we can frequently advise as to the best step to
take in a business matter which, if taken, will

bring in considerable material wealth. Just as we can influence in a spiritual sense, so we can influence in a business way. We people over here can see both sides of the argument When a thing is to be decided between two people we can see both points and can therefore see which is right, and if we play straight we throw our influence in with that, whether it is to the benefit of our earth friend, in a material sense, or not. If we do this, and our earth friend loses or suffers from it, we invariably make it up later in a different way. If we throw our influence against our conviction, only in order to help our earth friend, *we* pay for it here ourselves, and our earth friend, who hereby gains unjustifiably, pays for it later, either whilst on earth or when in spirit life He will have to make return sooner or later, there is no escape, it is automatic.

In saying we can and do influence people on earth, I do not propose to go into the precise process of how we work. It is near enough to say that you know how you influence each other on earth: here the result is the same—but that is a matter which each on of you will deal with individually later on, when your own change comes, therefore it is not of necessity or of interest to you to know now.

You have on earth a saying that "coming events cast their shadows before." This is a truth. They do cast their influences, and sensitive people can always register them and can often make a guess at their origin.

CHAPTER XI

PREMONITIONS

THERE are many superstitions and many reasons given to explain what is called "premonition," but in almost every instance it can be traced to telepathy; there are so many forms of mental sympathy.

The chief form of premonition is that concerning the death of another, friend or relation. Now, *always* that can be traced to telepathy. You will agree that perhaps the person about to pass on was not anticipating his death. It may have been through a sudden accident, and yet "so-and-so" had a certain sign—a premonition—so many days, or such and such a time, beforehand

To explain: Mr. A has had a premonition about the death of Mr. B. It is followed up later by an accident in which Mr. B is killed. The spirit friends who are interested in Mr. B have been in continual attendance upon him, and are watching him in order to be of use whenever possible; but they cannot make him do this or that with any certainty, they can only influence him one way or another. Now all the actions of Mr. B's life are

producing certain effects, some of which Mr B
himself is not at once conscious of. . . . His spirit
friends are, and they can see, a certain distance
ahead, what the results of these actions—the general routine of his life—will be. In this way they
can see ahead what is going to occur to Mr B,
and although they will do their utmost to guide
him they cannot *act* for him. He sets his own
destiny in motion and he alone can alter it. At
such a time, the spirit friends, realizing that Mr.
B is in physical danger, will do our utmost to di-
vert his actions and movements: sometimes they
are successful, but in this particular instance they
are not, and Mr. B meets his death. The influence
being used by the spirit people has created a dis-
turbance of thought-force around him and, although he was not conscious of it himself, his
friend Mr. A has registered it upon his mind and
it has reproduced itself in sleep, as a dream, or as
a vision built up by thought-power and material-
ized thought and from the physical strength of
Mr. B. Distance between A and B makes no difference

Premonitions concerning an arrangement
made which is afterwards not fulfilled are caused
by the influence of spirit friends trying always to
guide their charges to the benefit of themselves.
In this way you can figure out the cause of all so-
called premonitions. In every case it is spirit
friends trying to communicate with the person
chiefly concerned—he often fails to register what
another will pick up.

CHAPTER XII

RESIDENCE

I COME now to the last days on the Blue Island and the taking up of our residence on the next and far more permanent world. The Blue Island is a transient life; a land for acclimatising the new-comer, and as soon as he's fit, he passes from it to what I might term the Real World, inasmuch as each one will be much longer on it than any has yet been on earth. We can at will return to the Blue Island, and many do so frequently, both to meet newly-arrived friends and associates, and to help any person or group with whom we are in sympathy. These are only visits, and we do not ever again return there to live.

Travel here is a very different thing to the methods you all know, and we all set out in a large party for the Real World. Not our whole party, as on arrival; many were ready to leave, but with us were many other spirit people besides those with whom we had originally arrived. There was the same sensation of flying, moving rapidly

through the air; then we came to our new home.
After the colour and generally striking appearance
of the Blue Island, this new land appeared less at-
tractive at the outset. It was more toneless in
colour, the people more engrossed in their own
regular routine. It seemed as if we had returned
to earth life again, it was all so like. I think, on
arrival here, we must all have been attracted to
different parts of this land, for my own seemed
strikingly like parts I had known on earth, and
there was also buildings I knew. Other people
have told me the same, so I am confident that according to our race and degree of development so
we are automatically attracted to different parts
of this new world.

It is in this land that I and most of our people are, and certainly all will be, in due course.
We continue our studies and our work of develop-
ing spiritually, whilst at the same time controll-
ing and dispersing the few still-clinging earth
habits and thoughts. We are all very much more
conscious of each other in this land, and life re-
sumes a much greater similarity to the life we
have known on earth. We have our homes in the
same way and our interests in other people, and
according to taste so we are habited together in
houses or on the open hillside country. Some people live in very elaborate palaces, and it is very
curious to note that many of these people are
those who have led very rough and hard lives upon
earth. Their idea of Heaven is a place and a life
of ease. After a period of time, during which they

must make specified progress in general development, these people are given their places in order to allow them full advantage of environment to make forward steps in their evolution. If they don't progress, they lose their palace and must requalify for it. This applies to everyone, each has to qualify in order to obtain his desired object; and in order to keep it he must continue his progress and his help to others.

When we come to this land, we have ceased to desire food, drink and sleep; we are now pure spirit in the rough state; there is still more refining to be done in this next phase. Here, also, there are Rest Houses—Houses for Music—Houses for Scientific Research—Houses for all, and every kind of information and knowledge; and the entrance fee to each and all of these is Desire. We do not lead a life of continual cramming of information—we lead ordinary earth lives, but with a much keener social interest and much more freedom and exchange of thought. There is no distinction of the classes. Our earth life may be forgotten, in so far as our individual task on earth is concerned, when that task was a matter of little or no interest to us. It is only the spiritual and mental knowledge and development which hinders and advances the individual here; and spirit knowledge is not hindered by whatever one's job on earth may have been. In this respect there is a great and sudden broadening of the point of view of all comers to this land.

It is a land of freedom. A land of happiness and smiles. A land of happiness brought about through the real love of man for man A land to work for—a land in which your place is made according to the knowledge you have had whilst upon earth and the way you have used that knowledge.

It is impossible to over-emphasise the degree of freedom in this new world, or the joy each and all has in it.

In saying that your happiness is gauged by the knowledge acquired on earth and the application of that knowledge, I am saying what is accurate to the smallest detail, but I would like to explain percisely.

On being established here, in the Real World, each one is interviewed by one of the Advanced Spirit instructors and the whole record of earth is discussed and analysed. Reason, motive and result. The full and detailed record contains everything, there is nothing overlooked, and this is the time for paying the bill. Each is interviewed alone, and there is a minute analysis of all events, acts and thoughts. Then there is the making good to be gone through, the sum total to be paid . . . for all our thoughtlessness and our unkind acts and words—all that have had direct results must be paid for.

We have then to spend time in close touch with earth, in order, by influence, to make good for our past misdoings; make good as far as possible. Also we have the knowledge and full sight of the results of these earlier acts, and they do not bring happiness. But after that state is passed and we can bring all these things into proper perspective and form a table of work, which will gradually and continually be working out the results and troubles we have caused, then we can each one settle down to live here in freedom.

The form of life differs here enormously according to temperament, personality, and the influence of earth life. People vary in strange contrast to one another. Many of us carry on with our same work as on earth. Here we have no need to work in order to obtain daily livelihood, we work here solely for spiritual refinement and progress; at the same time we keep in touch with our earth interests as a form of recreation.

We are not always, without any break, in one house or another studying this, that and the other; we have a certain programme to go through but it has many breaks, and in this "off duty" time we come back to our dear people on earth, and either out of interest and love, or from the desire to be useful, we try our utmost to help them in their material and mental difficulties.

We have every form of recreation here, as I have already told you when dealing with the Blue Island. Any habit or hobby formed on earth can be indulged in here, always providing it is progressive.

From this you can understand that life after death is a very normal and natural affair. We have still our affections, and those which last are

still strongly binding links. Between families and
friends we have the same affections—and yet not
the same, because sometimes on earth there are
differences which cause a silence between members
of a family, and perhaps over here that family will
once more be very united—the earth differences
being based solely upon material things—once re-
move the material and the physical and underneath
the love often remains.

One great change which death brings is a
much broader point of view and a much larger
mind. A deeper understanding, a keener intuition,
clears away immediately many former difficulties
and misunderstandings. Once on this Real World,
and once passed the first initiation and payments
of debts, we are free to do as we wish, but we have
to progress or we ourselves curtail our liberties.
It is not an enforced progress, we can take our own
time about everything, but we must not allow any
of earth's instincts to increase in their power over
us. We have to learn the new conditions and live
for them entirely.

Once free we can travel over our own world
and over yours. So great is our speed and method
of travel that we can be in two places almost sim-
ultaneously.

Everywhere we go we are conscious of the
general love for another. It is much more evident
than on earth, and that great affection is the direct
cause of the general brightness and radiance of
this world. I do not mean that it gives off rays
of light, but rather that the general atmosphere is

light in quality and very invigorating and strength-giving.

Life here is a grander thing—a bolder thing, and a happier thing for all those who have led reasonable lives on earth, but for the unreason-able there are many troubles and difficulties and sorrows to be encountered. There is a great truth in the saying that "as ye sow, so shall ye reap."

CHAPTER XIII

GENERAL RESULTS

I HAVE been away from earth life now a number of years, and although I have been in constant and unbroken touch with my old conditions and affections, I have never, since leaving the Blue Island, had any desire to return to the earth for habitation.

There have been many occasions when I have very badly wanted a tongue for a few hours. With my extra sight I have known the right treatment when seeing certain situations being mishandled. At such times I have very badly wanted to return to earth for an hour, in order to be the means of bringing about great improvements—beyond these passing desires I have had no wish ever to take up residence on earth; my travels and my works and studies on this side of the grave have been of such vital interest. Since being here I have acquired greater knowledge, and have been able to pass to earth people *some* of that knowledge, at different times.

Ever since my leaving the world, your world, I have been keenly interested in its developmnet, and very alive to all its internal and external difficulties. Patriotism still holds with me, as with most of us, and will continue to hold so long as I have personal ties upon earth. When there are no longer any of these personal ties remaining, my interests will gradually and naturally turn more exclusively to *this* side among my own people, and my place will be filled by another—and so the race goes on—always moving forward, progressing and evolving.

Looking back on it all since I first came to the Blue Isle, I have great satisfaction in seeing the advance I have made. Coming here was quite a shock to me. I had no idea that my death was so near when that particular year began, and I certainly had no desire that it should be soon. I had an overwhelming number of important things on my hands. Some of these I have been able to finish since, and I have followed the progress of many others. Soon after arrival I had grown acclimatised to the new conditions, the new appearance of everything, the new power of locomotion and communication. We do not talk to each other very much here, we have a more expressive and intimate way than that. Here, thoughts are communicated from one mind to another without the need of vocal expression, although we *can* talk in earth manner at will.

There are, of course, many and vast differences between my world and yours, but I always find one of the most blessed and merciful differences between the two to be the manner in which the mental is unhindered by the physical. You on earth have mental desires and ambitions of various kinds, for money, success in business, pleasure, power, knowledge, etc.; but always these desires are limited, cramped, often made impossible owing to your physical condition—here, when the mental desire is good, the field is unlimited. Any mental desire for truth, knowledge, be it what it may, can be gratified in a most astonishing manner in *this* world. Be it good or bad, it will bring its results, and if the desire is bad, it will grow in power and must be paid for; if good it will grow in power also, and will bring strength and happiness with it.

I cannot emphasise to you too much, that as *you are*, so *you will be*.

You are now, whilst on earth, making your bodies for your next conditions. These are built up by your present lives and the quality of your thoughts. This world which I have been in a long time now, is the closest thing imaginable to your earth. It is full of mineral, vegetable, animal, and *all* forms of life. All the animals you have loved on earth and educated to understanding, will be with you here. Those other animals who belong to no one in particular are here too, but they are in their own places. You will say, "Oh, then it is only a reflection of your world." It is not that way— the earth is only a reflection of *this* world. Earth is not the lasting world. It is the training school. You are not only on earth to amass riches and

enjoy the life, just for what it is; you are there
to learn the truth about your own character, and
how to control and develop it, to make full use of
all earth's beauties and pleasures, BUT you must
be master, and do not allow them to master you.

As I have said, looking back on my life here,
I am satisfied with what has been done both in the
personal and individual way *and* the bigger way.
We spirit people have made great advances in our
communications with earth. We have been greatly and enormously helped by the physical strength
of the spirits of all the young men and women
who passed over during the recent fighting all over
the world; not only English, but all. They brought
with them great physical power and determina-
tion, and we have been able, through this power,
to break down many of the barriers which kept
the two worlds apart.

These truths do not conform with the ideas
of many people, but that is no reason for saying
they are not true. Truth is sometimes unexpected
and none too pleasant, but it is always the most
powerful, and *will* make itself known—no matter whether it brings pleasure or pain.

Go, each one of you, in reality or imagination,
to the edge of a high cliff overlooking the sea.
Let it be a bright, starry, frosty night, and go
alone. Stand there and meditate. Look down upon the lights of any harboured, anchored boats,
and think; then look up to the stars. You know
where you are, and you are fully conscious of the
flickering and movement of the lights on the boats.

You can see them. You are only a little way off . . . and perhaps you could make them hear if you called, but it would be easier to wait till the darkness breaks when they can see you without any effort on your part. That is how we spirit people are; conscious of those left behind, some willing to wait, others fighting and struggling to make themselves heard. It is only a little way from earth, and betwen this, our spirit state and the Great Ultimate, there is as much distance as between you on the cliff and the farthest star.

We are only a little way on our journey— nothing yet forgotten. Love still remaining.

CHAPTER XIV

THE GREAT ULTIMATE

MY LIFE here has been a very normal, healthy and interesting affair, just as my life on earth was. I have been invested with no powers generally attributed to spirits and fairies, I am still just an ordinary man with an ordinary plain, blunt outlook on life; the change has in no way altered me. The only change there is in me is my greater ability to move speedily and act quickly. I am rejuvenated, and this is a condition which boomes more marked as time goes on.

Many people who give thought to these subjects, no matter what their particular point of of view may be, ask the question, "To where is all leading? What is to be our ultimate state?" This is a question of extreme difficulty to deal with on account of the limitations of the mind; both yours and ours.

I have explained to you that as you are, so you will be when you come here. When here you you will qualify for a further state, which will be

your lot in due time, and there you will be exactly
as you have made yourself by your life *here*. Better
or worse, happier or more unhappy. From that
you will go to a further state, another sphere if
you like, and there again you will have made your
own conditions.

In this further state you will be more self-
contained; a word I use to express a state of being
less dependent upon other people and things for
development and progress. In this sphere you
will again come in contact with your *whole record*.
A record in full, of all former states: and from
this sphere, if your record has qualified to the point
of allowing it, you will be given the choice of re-
turning to earth again. Reincarnating. If your
record does not qualify for *choice* in the matter,
you will be *directed* either to return or to continue, according to what the Teachers—the Purified—consider will afford you most opportunity
for re-creating yourself and cleansing yourself in
the necessary way. It is from this sphere that
spirits return to earth; but by the time the most
progrssed spirit has reaached this state he has
forgotten in detail his association with earth. I
cannot give the shortest period of time which
would be necessary to reach this sphere, but the
sojourn in the Real World after the Blue Island
is a much longer period than that of mortal life;
and in each sphere as progress is made the sojourn is *longer*.

The spirits who have reached this "Return
or Stay Sphere," and are purified and qualified in

themselves, those who stand the tests and pass out
as Grade 1, pass to another and altogether different
and lighter land—and each becomes impersonal.
Impersonal in the sense that they are no longer
Jack Brown or Madge Black, they are now pure
spirit people, and their former love, which had been
a personal and individual thing, is no longer for
one equally for all. All are alike to all. The pur-
est tissue of God Love binds one and all.

I have given a brief outline, sufficient for you
to form your own ideas, your own mental pictures
of Creation and its process. There would be no
point in my going further into details, because
if I were to give the facts you could not understand the conditions ruling in those advanced
states. I am not able fully to understand them
myself, for as I have said, I am only a little way
on my journey, but just far enough to grasp the
intense beauty of life, and in life.

As one standing on a higher point than
yourselves, and able to see a little more than you
see, I can best explain to you that in these future
states you receive not merely fifty, or sixty, or even
a hundred per cent. out of your lives in happiness
and joy, but you receive comparatively six hundred
per cent. This is simply a graphic way of indicat-
ing the degree of happiness that obtains here.
Were I able to describe all the processes of our
evolution many would say, "Oh, but I don't want
that!" But when progress has been made and intelligence brightened and Reality seen as Reality,
not as Imagination, they will want it. If I said to

an old man in an invalid chair that he could have a motor bicycle, he'd say he preferred his invalid chair, but if he were to be a young, robust boy of nineteen again, which do you suppose he'd choose? This is the underlaying principle.

Do not think that this scheme of the World is hateful and unkind and full of continual partings from all other spirits who are dear to each individally. I have said that there are *no* partings. It is always possible and customary for spirits to keep in close touch with each other on this side. When the highest states of the impersonal are reached there are no partings from dear ones; only a wider opening of that same door of love—a higher, purer love, a Golden or God love, to admit not one or two or twenty, but to embrace ALL.

CHAPTER XV

CHRIST AND SPIRITUALISM

UNFORTUNATELY the word "spiritualism" has been associated with so many misconceptions that it affords scope for misinterpretations and, for this reason, thousands of people misunderstand the word and suppose that it deals only with forms of fortune-telling, and chicanery of all kinds, and must necessarily be wrong and dangerous—therefore the work of anti-Christ. For this reason it is a barred subject. Not only do these people know nothing about it but they are so horrified at the travesty they themselves have created that they would refuse to hear, see, or read a word upon the subject.

To all people who have knowledge of spiritualism, this attitude is tiresome and regrettable; nevertheless it exists to-day, and in great force.

In my concluding chapter I want to say a few simple words on this point.

Spiritualism is not the work of anti-Christ. All the teachings of Christ are to be found in the teachings of Spiritualism. Christ taught love amongst mankind, generous thought and generous help for one another. "Love thy neighbour as thyself," and so on. Spiritualism teaches these same doctrines. Christ was imbued with the Divine

Spirit, and He laid down laws upon which His disciples were to model their lives and their work, and in those laws you will find the laws which govern spiritualism.

Because one of the disciples was a dishonest, weak man, and because some of the workers since then, workers in the churches of various and many creeds have been, and are to this day, weak and sinful in their lives, you do not, any of you, think for one moment that the whole is bad and evil. You realize that the teachings of Christ were of the highest. Always He spoke of Love as the building link and the force of all good. I want you to understand, perhaps for the first time, that spiritualism is based upon the same foundations. All its rules are the rules by Christ Himself. All the creeds existing upon the earth are based upon these same rules. They vary in minor points considerably. What one will allow another will condemn, and it is for the individual to decide which particular one of all is most fitted to himself. By his choice he will show his ability to grasp the meaning of God's laws, and according to his development so will he select.

The teachings of all alike are limited but some go farther, see farther, and understand more. Just as all roads may converge to a given point, so many creeds follow in the main the teachings of Christ. Some by narrow little roads and byways, some by wide roads, and some by main highways. Spiritualism is God's Main Highway.

THE END